SATISFIED
WITH
HAVOC

SATISFIED WITH HAVOC

poems by ~~Jo McDougall~~

Jo McDougall (signature)

Autumn House Press

PITTSBURGH

"Autumn House" and "Autumn House Press" are registered trademarks owned by Autumn House Press, a non-profit corporation whose mission is the publication and promotion of poetry.

Cover photograph: Carla Shapiro
Author photograph: Tom Dawson, Skipworth Inc.
Text and cover design: Kathy Boykowycz
Editorial Consultant: Eva Maria Simms
Community Outreach Director: Michael Wurster
Media Consultant: Jan Beatty
Marketing Consultant: Jack Wolford
Associate Publisher: Susan Hutton

Printed in the U.S.A. by Thomson-Shore
ISBN: 0966941993
Library of Congress Control Number: 2004100856

For
Jadyn and Logan Elisabeth

and
in memory of Mary Laura

THE AUTUMN HOUSE POETRY SERIES

Michael Simms, editor

OneOnOne by Jack Myers

Snow White Horses, Selected Poems 1973-1988 by Ed Ochester

The Leaving, New and Selected Poems by Sue Ellen Thompson

Dirt by Jo McDougall

Fire in the Orchard by Gary Margolis

Just Once, New and Previous Poems by Samuel Hazo

The White Calf Kicks by Deborah Slicer
   (Winner of the 2003 Autumn House Poetry Prize, selected by
   Naomi Shihab Nye)

The Divine Salt by Peter Blair

The Dark Takes Aim by Julie Suk

Satisfied with Havoc by Jo McDougall

ACKNOWLEDGMENTS

Grateful acknowledgment is made to the editors of the following publications in which these poems, some in different versions, have appeared or will appear:

The Arkansas Democrat-Gazette: "Things"
The Arkansas Review: "Ashes," "History," "Hope"
Controlled Burn: "The Crows of Mica Street," "New Couple on the Block"
The Georgia Review: "Strangers in This City Where We Have Come Seeking a Cure for Her Cancer, My Daughter and I Drive Up to the Clinic," "The Widow Speaks"
Louisiana Literature: "Mothers and Daughters"
The Midwest Quarterly: "Blackbird"
The Morning News, Springdale, AR: "Snow in Arkansas"
Natural Bridge: "The Boys from Brewer Bottoms," "A Woman Speaks of Blue Skies" (as "Blue Skies")
New Century North American Poets/ River King Poetry Press: "Cloud's Lake" (as "Snow Lake"), "Gurney" (as "At Mercy Hospital"), "The Wait"
New Letters: "Arkansas," "A Bottomlands Farmer Remembers a Ball-peen Hammer"
North American Review: "Visiting My Daughter"
Pebble Lake Review: "Straightpins"
Perihelion: "At Frog's Trailer Court"
Salamander: "Oaks," "Snow in a New Hampshire Spring," "Watching a Grandson Play Little League Ball the Day Ted Williams Died"
Today's Alternative News: "Rumors"

Ongoing gratitude goes to Charles—my husband, friend, and valued critic. Thanks to Eva and Michael Simms, Autumn House Press, for their patient and perceptive editing; Sue Abbott Boyd, Kelly Cherry, Miller and Jordan Williams for their long history of support; Sam Hazo, Maryalice Hurst, M.J. Melneck, Tom and Jeanie Wilson for going the extra mile; Susan David, Gerald Stern, Robert Swaim, Susan Taylor, Jay White for their valuable suggestions for this manuscript.

Grateful acknowledgment is made to The MacDowell Colony and the Arkansas Arts Council for a 2004 residency and a 2003 fellowship, respectively, thereby advancing my work.

CONTENTS

II

I

STRANGER

New in town,
I'm sitting at the counter in Marge's Grill,
hiding behind a magazine,
reading about a man whose job is stitching corpses
in a funeral home.
The talk around me is of rain,
if it won't or will,
a losing Little League,
the farm show.

I think of the farm I grew up on,
the one nobody here would know;
the clarity of the moons,
quartered or halved or full,
hauling themselves up from behind the sheds.

In a dazzling moment of estrangement,
I leave my money on the counter,
cool to my touch

MARRIED

Tonight I ask my husband to help me remember
names for the breeds of chickens
he and I grew up with, living on neighboring farms.
From the far, tall grasses he calls them:
　　Wyandottes. Dominiques. Barred Rocks.
　　Rhode Island Reds. Silver Spangled Hamburgs.
　　Leghorns. Anconas. Buff Orpingtons....
"Mother used to call them 'Buff Orphans,'" I interrupt.
We laugh. He remembers my mother.
Evening settles itself,
whispering snow.
The kitchen nightlight makes a tiny moon
on the wall.

AFTER LOSING A CHILD

A man and a woman sit on the deck
in afternoon light.
She pushes back her chair.
He moves closer to catch her voice.
Dusk leafs absently through the trees.
They listen to whippoorwills
stitch and unstitch the same seam
in the dark.

WATCHING A GRANDSON PLAY LITTLE LEAGUE BALL THE DAY TED WILLIAMS DIED

(for Merritt)

It is late afternoon.
All over America, this scene:
distant traffic, the sound of the evening train,
parents calling out their children's names.

MOTHERS AND DAUGHTERS

When I was a child,
my mother and I traveled the long miles
to see her mother, once a year.
That hillside farm was mostly gravel,
the kitchen smelled like a churn,
guineas and chickens strutted the porch.
When we left,
my grandmother would stand
in her garden and wave.
I'd watch her a long time,
leaning out the window of the car.
My mother would say little on the way home,
her eyes now and then filling with tears.
Perhaps she was thinking of that garden,
the one she tried to replicate year after year,
every last pole bean and zinnia,
the one she left to me.

The 3 p.m. August heat
seeps under the cars,
whipping the dogs,
baking the trailers
like loaves of bread.

A woman using the park's public phone
wipes away the sweat,
fixing her eyes on a spot just above the asphalt
where for her, perhaps, the heat assumes
a familiar shape—a turtle, say, or a heron.
The heron might be blue,
standing in cool water.

SILENCE

(for Barry Strauss)

Older in these winter days,
I yearn less and less for silence.
I welcome the faucet's protest
in the room above mine,
the heavy tread of someone
late perhaps to work.

I look out on a meadow.
The deer, where are they?
It is not enough to see their tracks,
where they wandered yesterday.
I need the flick of their bodies
snapping a twig,
the chuff of their breath.

The sun slips down,
reluctant to disappear,
the way sound dims a room
when we turn off a radio.

WORK

(for Miller and Jordan Williams)

It is summer, dusk.
Sitting with your wife on the lawn,
you think of the day's work you have done,
how you lowered yourself into it slowly,
as a coffin might enter a grave.
Work is good, the crickets promise.
The cicadas agree.
The worm makes no noise,
busy about its chiseling.
In the sudden quiet,
the faint scratch of hooves—
as if a horse you'd known as a child
were cantering round a nearby field.

Your heart settles itself
like moon upon water
as you regard the dark,
the work yet to be done,
the woman beside you.
Against a blackening sky,
fireflies dim.

THE HOUSE ON LAKE ICE ROAD

Sunlight jimmies its way
through the dusty windows.
On the kitchen table
one orange leans against the blue sky of a bowl
where someone has dropped a mitten,
keys, a greasy sack.
My friend pours the coffee;
I clear a space for the cups.
I want this never to change.
The clock
(Big Ben, red hands, 1930s plastic)
dutifully erases our every word.

THE WAIT

A buzzard riding thermals
above a pine beside a Louisiana highway
spots the carcass of a small dog
left by a speeding car.
It is mid-July. A gossamer of trembling
alerts the buzzard's spine.
Here is an odor with promise.
Soon the air will turn to an oily shimmer,
a texture of such velvet and exquisite heft
that the buzzard contents himself to wait,
rocking night after night in the arms of the pine.

PAYING ATTENTION

Coming home to visit my parents' graves,
I enter the house where I was born.
My mother sits at a table, sewing,
her eyes a deepening blue.
My father comes in from the fields.
Until now I have never known
that intent young man,
that slender woman
who lean toward each other
and touch hands
and rise together to climb the stairs,
long vistas of the fields dissolving
as dusk puts down its roots.

HONEYMOON

On their way home from the honeymoon
("fantastic weekend, heart shaped tub,
breathtaking views"),
they stop at a run-down motel.
She hadn't realized he'd be so
economical.
She hopes there's more than one towel,
that the sheets are clean,
that he won't say the things, as he did last night,
to make her cry,
things not unlike
what her father used to say to her mother
as she listened from the dark of the stairs.

Sometime in the night
she hears a woman sobbing in the next room.
Moonlight papers the walls.
She thinks of every ramshackle house
her father moved them in and out of.

Just before sleep,
she glimpses herself in a far corner,
brushing her hair,
rehearsing something she'll say at first light
to make her husband make a fist.

SNOW

When God created snow,
He melted down coyote, wolf,
eagle, wolverine, fisher, fox
into a darkness
that falls when it chooses,
decked out in trickster white,
that tracks us,
curious and aloof,
wanting a key,
a scarf,
breath.

THE AUNTS

(for Victor Girerd)

In Charleroi, Belgium,
they stand in front of the family home,
arms linked,
as someone takes this photograph
dated 1952.
They are three:
Amelia, a spy for the resistance,
imprisoned by the Germans in World War I;
Augusta, my father's mother,
who ran away to America at seventeen;
Marie, who helped her in that deceit.

These years later,
defiant in smart hats and suits,
they study me,
clearly disappointed.

WALKING IN WOODS

Lift the forest floor, slightly.
Be aware of what is hiding,
going about its business
in the silky chambers of itself.
And should that creature shyly one day
come to you,
or a bird cut out a song from the papery sky
and float it toward you,
think it neither by your cunning
nor your grace
that the world happened to tip its hat—a lilt, a shadow—
as you happened to pass.

Last night, alone in the kitchen,
I felt my dead mother brush my sleeve.
She wasn't smiling. She didn't say
How are you, How are the kids?
She was, I have to say it, rude.
Talking to the dead,
you can't be sure they hear.
You tell yourself they do,
that they're merely distracted,
doing their best to fit in
to the sweet bye and bye.

You wonder if it's hard to make friends there,
if now that they're nothing but air
they stumble over things,
how they cope with never saying words
like *foxglove* or *nasturtium* again.

THE SLIGHT

From the wooded swale
behind the house,
the last of the snow
has come to die,
ghosts of it rising,
sifting north along a ridge.

Although they've ventured perilously close,
it's clear they have no use for us,
nodding among themselves,
turning their backs,
going about their business.

We, too, return to our tasks—sorting potatoes,
mending a sock—
miffed and oddly out of sorts.

DRIVING HIGHWAY 71

Gliding into sleep,
I caught myself just before crossing
the center line.
At that moment a hawk,
alert to something on the highway,
dove perilously close to my left wheel.
As he corrected,
as sunlight powered his decision,
I saw at my left hand
the silver underside of his wing.

Shouldn't there have been cymbals,
a crescendo of sound?
A sea had parted to let us pass,
closing behind us
with scarcely a flicker.

TO MY DAUGHTER, WHO REFUSES
TO MEET ME HALFWAY

As implacable as my mother's garden
jelled in moonlight,
as silent as the dog who disappeared forever
down a dusty lane,
the dead remain estranged.
Daily they recede,
seeking the more distant stars.

Dating our lives from their departures,
we beg them for signs.
We want to stumble upon them napping
or peeling an orange.
They send nothing, no nearer to us now
than the day they nodded to Death
and asked him in.

DUMB

You would think the dog,
lemon-sized brain notwithstanding,
would understand by now
that the truck with the broken muffler
passing down our street each night
is not his master's truck
and will not turn into our driveway;
the familiar key will not undress itself
in our lock.
Still, he bounds to the door
at the muffler's first faint cough.
Thus hope outfoxes reason,
the dog and I growing dumber by the week.

II

THE CROWS OF MICA STREET

Their calls grate
like shears cutting heavy tin.
Misfits among the robins and wrens,
they flock to this street,
stolid as midwives on their rounds.
I receive their song in my ruined life
like scalding water in a new wound.
I walk on, redeemed.

STRAIGHTPINS

Growing up in a small town,
we didn't notice
the background figures of our lives,
gray men, gnarled women,
dropping from us silently
like straightpins to a dressmaker's floor.
The old did not die
but simply vanished
like discs of snow on our tongues.
We knew nothing then of nothingness
or pain or loss—
our days filled with open fields,
football,
turtles and cows.

One day we noticed
Death has a musty breath,
that some we loved
died dreadfully,
that dying
sometimes takes time.

Now, standing in a supermarket line
or easing out of a parking lot,
we realize
we've become the hazy backgrounds
of younger lives.
How long has it been,
we ask no one in particular,
since we've seen a turtle
or a cow?

NEW COUPLE ON THE BLOCK

We give them a week
to settle in.
We ask them over to a neighborhood buffet.

She is talkative; he is aloof.
Over dessert, someone asks him
"What is it you do?"
He says he builds houses.
He says the last one was made
of pink corrugated cardboard,
surrounded by a moat.
Landscaped, of course.
The men murmur politely
and study their plates.

I look at our guest.
He's leaning back,
savoring his wine.
I think I understand
how he survives.

PRISTINE

It's what we want—
the antique's impeccable provenance,
the surround smell of the new car,
sheets just out of the wash.
In this room
the walls are white,
waiting for the moon.
I think of the city I have left,
its sirens, its Wal-Marts,
its viper streets.
Looking out into woods
that take scarce note of this window,
I think of caribou
crossing first snow.

CLOUD'S LAKE

The summer Sammy Erickson drowned
we were fifteen, immortal.
When we heard they couldn't find the body,
we buried his memory
like a contentious bone.
We knew the lake he'd drowned in;
it was our silvery world.
We laid our blankets down beside it,
built small fires and counted stars.
We ignored the razors of glass
nightly sharpening themselves along the shore,
the stuttering codes
glinting off the water.
Picnics, white sails, our young bodies
obscured the docks' slow rot,
stumps rising under speeding boats
like sharks,
the bones of Sammy Erickson
turning the wrong way home.

SNOW IN A NEW HAMPSHIRE SPRING

Snow, my boon companion,
my rock of ages,
my delight, my destroyer,
my church, my foundation—
who has redeemed the earth
and swept away the stench of dead leaves—
you are shrinking, melting
down to your grave.
Even now
you succumb to the grass
storming the hill,
its young and ignorant body
wild to take everything.

Coach Danner loved them.
With those boys on the team
our high school won All-District in football
every year.
Coach never told them what to do. They knew.
They'd grown up
defending their fathers' stills.
They knew every shortcut in those swamps and woods
to outfox the sheriff and his dogs.
The town doctor said
when he was sent for by one of them
somebody would meet him at the highway
and take him in by boat.
They always made sure
he saw the rifle.

We heard they lived in shacks and ate snakes.
We heard all strangers disappeared
without a trace.
On the football field
envy and moonshine drove their brains.
They hated the town boys,
whose fathers worked

and drank coffee every morning
with the sheriff and the chief of police.
They were handsome and polite,
respected their elders,
could crack a man's back,
their blue eyes smiling.

TAKEN

Doing battle with the fly swatter and the Raid,
I stun the red rambunctious wasp
cavorting in my den.
It stutters and simmers. It grows still.
Remorse sets in.
What if I, dancing one night
alone in my room,
should catch the ever roving eye of God
and be struck down,
dispatched like a gnat,
God being God and marginally annoyed?

FLYING OVER THE SCABLANDS, SEATTLE TO PULLMAN

(for Paula Coomer)

As we climb,
I see a glass lake,
a desert marked with dead waves,
dots of forests
green as Astroturf.

If we go down,
we may fall into those cardboard trees,
those scablands thin as snakeskin,
that bored lake
which may or may not extinguish
our inconvenient flames.

A BOTTOMLANDS FARMER REMEMBERS
A BALL-PEEN HAMMER

He was the master of it, my father was,
killing snakes with it, battening shingles down,
threatening the convicts the prison sent him, summers,
to pull Johnson grass out of the fields.
It wasn't the hammer made me afraid that day
when, spitting my name, he came at me,
stopping himself as he drew back his arm—
but the set of his jaw,
his knuckles white as gristle
as he threw the hammer down,
his eyes rid of me forever.

A WOMAN TIRES OF HEARING ACORNS ON THE ROOF

All October they have dinged our roof
like berserk goats.

Today my doctor has phoned.
The tests have come back positive;
he'll see me in his office
tomorrow.

Hungry now for snow to lay down
its quiet tarpaulins,
I recall the dirt I was instructed to scatter
as a child, how it rang
on my grandfather's lowered coffin.

DANCE

(in memory of Agha Shahid Ali)

Shahid would say, if he had lived to see
another spring,
A bird on a far ridge
recalling how a song is sung,
the tap dances of mice
between the walls,
the thickening air of fireflies
and flies—
Why not be happy?

The tulips and jonquils,
begonias and lilies—
upstarts of color,
arrogant shills,
silly to the core—
the petulant ambulance
which has not yet turned
down my street.

Come dance with me.

HISTORY

Our parents told us stories
from the Great Depression:
my father's mother hiding her last dollar
in the garden
under the second plant
in the second row of spinach,
my mother's cousin
found hanged by his Sunday necktie
in the kitchen
after the factory laid him off.

These stories bumped our lives
like old-maid aunts coming to visit—
exotic, worrisome, finally gone—
while our parents struggled to provide us
with packaged bread,
clean underwear,
sidewalks lined with pink and purple phlox.

BALANCE

After you're gone,
after the children have rifled through your things,
the papers and paperweights,
the policies and pewter pigs,
all will be factored in,
deducted from your balance—
how you took ten photos of one grandchild
at Christmas
and only five and two of the others,
the letters you forgot to burn—
and, to your credit, your request
that equal numbers of the Sunday dishes
go to everyone.

Then the children will return to their lives
slighted and scorned,
arguing for years
over who should get this button,
that cracked comb.

BLACKBIRD

It's been over forty years.
On a monotonous highway in November rain
the car in front of me
vanished and entered the world again
upside down in a field.
A man and a woman lay in the stubble wheat.

    As if in a movie,
    I see myself kneel beside them
    to cover the woman with my coat.
    They say nothing, staring at the sky.
    The *kong-ka-ree, kong-ka-ree* of a red-winged
      blackbird
    rings out;
    then I hear the silence.

Memory brightens the scene that day
when the world shattered in a breath—
my yellow coat against the brown field,
the trickle of red from the woman's lips,
the gray and distant trees,
the blackbird, its crimson epaulets,
the song that came to live in my brain
and has never slept.

41

TARANTULA

Walking the dog,
I see an out-of-round paper cup
wobbling like a tarantula
down the hill.

I am five.
My grandmother's voice fills the world.
"Get back! Get back!" she shouts
as a black shape advances over the rocks.
Later she tells me the spider's name.

Longing dumbfounds me: that house, those rocks, her face,
the bowl with the one wax pear
catching dust on the kitchen table.

MAMMOGRAM

"They're benign," the radiologist says,
pointing to specks on the x ray
that look like dust motes
stopped cold in their dance.
His words take my spine like flame.
I suddenly love
the radiologist, the nurse, my paper gown,
the vapid print on the dressing room wall.
I pull on my radiant clothes.
I step out into the Hanging Gardens, the Taj Mahal,
the Niagara Falls of the parking lot.

TAXIDERMY

Let us mourn the giraffe and zebra,
dead during heavy bombardment
in a Gaza Strip zoo—
one of terror,
one of tear gas.
There is no money to replace them,
so they will be stuffed
and put back in their cages
for children to see
how it was when these were animals—
although someone who can remember
will have to explain
how the brusque tails sent flies reeling;
how, like barley in an evening wind,
they bent their necks to water;
how the eyes were not glass then,
and darker.

IN THE CRITICAL CARE WAITING ROOM

(in memory of Ray and Mary Faver)

The next of kin live in the green befores:
before the fall, the stroke, the mugger's knife,
cancer's knavery, the clot, battered doors
of the heart. Hope, doctors, strategies for buying
time consume their lives. They despise the blood,
tubes, smells, each day's descent into Hell—
while a soft rain, the notes of a thrush
remind them spring is rising somewhere else;
somewhere someone is dancing a tango. They lose
keys, cars, good jackets, mail; make lists
and forget them; smile for the stricken father, spouse,
child; try not to think of the Apocalypse.
    In waiting they find order, all order gone,
      their porch lights at noon burning absently on.

STRANGERS IN THIS CITY WHERE WE HAVE COME
SEEKING A CURE FOR HER CANCER,
MY DAUGHTER AND I DRIVE UP TO THE CLINIC

A buzzard lands on the roof.
In the dusk, in my confusion,
I mistake it for a blue
heron. I call to my daughter, "Look!"

COMA

In this place
even your name won't keep you
from being anonymous.
When the nurse comes in,
I list your attributes:
witty, smooth dancer,
devoted to the dog.
Look, I want to shout, This is my friend.
This is who he is.
I take from my wallet your photograph
in the absurd blue tux.
The nurse nods politely,
but her eye is on the sparrows
of your chart,
drab waves and dots.

You lie lost,
your blood turned to shadow.
When the nurse isn't looking,
I close your fingers
over a strand of the dog's hair.

AFTER ALL IS SAID AND DONE

For all kind thoughts and all memorials,
we send forth thank-you notes,
rage and love and ashes
in paper boats.

DISSATISFIED LIFE

Taller than the emptied house beside it,
a tree climbs, decade after decade,
quibbling with heaven, waiting
for the cat to pour himself again across the grass,
the daily paper to thunk at sunup in the drive,
the woman to step out in the mornings,
yawning, cursing the rickety stoop.

SNOW IN ARKANSAS

Paltry as measles,
it flirts with the ground—
a diva among the awe-struck,
heady with success,
warmly received.
When it comes to town,
schools close in its honor,
drivers sacrifice their cars
before the altar of the white ditch.
Then snow withdraws its troops,
satisfied with the havoc,
the rave reviews,
gone on up north
to be with its people.

THE ONLY COLOR BLUE SHOULD BE

Living in Kansas,
I didn't feel the buffalo through the soles of my shoes,
didn't see in its sky
the only color blue should be,
didn't step into the sunshine
glancing like God's grace off the Missouri.
Yet, held apart from me now
by several states,
Kansas rises in my bones
like a first love
or cancer.

Taking respite from her husband's slow dying,
she joins us late.
We babble of war and politics,
horses, children, art.
She keeps a slight distance
as if we were a spectator sport.
Her eyes darken
with the memory of his body, perhaps,
as she laughs at someone's story
volleyed across the white cloth.

GURNEY

My daughter lies in the last stage
of her disease.
Making my way
to her hospital room,
I meet a gurney, empty I assume,
until I see the small rise in the covering sheet
where a nose would be.
I know a body is there,
or what is left of one.

I enter her room.
Fighting for my life,
I water the flowers on the windowsill.

DOMINION

Such youth, beauty, power—
the first time snow causes a moose to fall
or a house;
the first time it takes a farm,
a town, whole states.
Then the thirst to be exalted
in Psalter and paean and ode,
even in prose;
to be lauded for its purity
under a granite moon,
to be feared for its dominion
as far as the crow can see.

Then the slow decline, as sure
as Rome's:
the ruinous warming of the ground,
the vengeful, first spring rains,
the Nazi sun,
thinning ranks, skirmishes,
untidy retreats to the north sides of trees.
Then prayers for reinforcements: cold air from Canada,
black ice, a thumping freeze.

Banished from its fiefdoms, the bastions
it so recently pillaged and raped,
snow lies down in rags,
wasted, its color gone bad.
And no one to pay a last respect,
no one to grieve,
no one to mark the bonny fields
of its surrender,
to say one day to visitors
Here. Here is the grave.

PARALLEL LIVES

I've become the guardian of my daughter's jewelry
until her daughters come of age.
These rings, a brooch,
a stone or two
are what they'll touch
as her body turns to lace.

A YOUNG WIDOWER REMEMBERS

As I watched life leave her body,
I thought of country songs we used to dance to,
how the steel guitar slid the music down,
sizzling
to the last note. We lingered,
as hesitant to leave the dance floor,
the harmonica,
each other
as early morning fog to leave a river.

VISITING MY DAUGHTER

For weeks
I visited every day,
drawn to that fresh rise,
the blister of her grave.

THINGS

These things I hold more dearly now—
breath. Green grass. My husband's
laugh. Chocolate. Hydrangeas. Keys.
Islands off the coast of Maine.
And this dog,
who never tires
of owning me,
who lets me enter every morning
the clear lakes of his eyes.

THE WIDOW SPEAKS

It's been six months. Everybody is kind
for awhile. I've given away some of his shoes.
I ought to call Goodwill to come for the suits;
none of the children want them, and it's time.

Here's something I've learned: The dead live on in us
their ordinary lives, not knowing they've changed.
If spoken to while drinking their coffee, they may look up.
It's not enough, but something. Try not to complain.

A WOMAN SPEAKS OF BLUE SKIES

You and I meet again by chance.
All evening we are giddy,
puffed up like pigeons.
You call the next day
but your words drag their feet.
I hang up the phone. I look out the window.
The sky is blue,
bored as a bone.

HOPE

The man waiting for a transplant,
the woman waiting for the chemo to work,
the boy in the projects
waiting for a bike

have all spotted Hope,
that great bird
who may sweep them up,
let them ride between his snowy wings.

It's a long flight.
He tires easily.
Someone will have to be
shaken off.

SUITCASES

I'd like not to be a migratory bird,
passion to passion,
saying, too often, goodbye.
I'd like to put these suitcases deep away,
never feel again
their closing sound inside me.

I want to open, summer, winter, summer
the same front door,
feel the same key
dozing in my pocket.

MOTHER'S DAY

I water the red impatiens,
the strawflowers and dahlias bordering the lawn.
I lean against the moss-covered bricks
of the house.
I think of the cemetery
where my daughter lies buried young,
orphaned of her children,
incredulous
among those sullen graves.

ASHES

Passing beside the fireplace,
last night's cold fire,
I note a rustling,
as if a wasp were dozing itself awake
inside the morning paper
or a ghost had thought
of something I need to know.

OAKS

When friends came,
bringing food and sympathy,
I asked them to speak of my daughter
in the present tense.

When I visited her grave,
the oak trees,
casting their ferny shadows,
set me straight.

ARKANSAS

They came in a sizzling 1950s August
to the back door,
three black men raising money
for a black college.
In dark hats and suits,
stepping out of a car
polished like a Steinway,
they made their polite case,
then backed out of the slow drive
raising not a mote of dust.
Past broken tractors and scorched fields,
past farmers cursing God and sprockets,
they floated in that impeccable car,
erect as pharaohs.

RUMORS

Once, the house I grew up in
glowed like a Hopper painting,
white paint intact,
its porch light waiting up for me.
Alive now only in my mind,
it is dying—and everything in it,
rumors of shapes
like faces in a photograph
left too long on a sunny table.